Unlock A Better Life: The Amazing Benefits of Living Your Life With Purpose

By

Kristine J. Summers

Unlock A Better Life By Kristine J. Summers

Copyright © [2023] by Kristine J. Summers.

Disclaimer

The information in this book is provided for general informational and educational purposes only and is not a substitute for professional advice. While the author has made every effort to ensure that the information provided is accurate and up to date, **Kristine J. Summers** makes no representations or warranties of any kind, express or implied, about the completeness, accuracy, reliability, suitability, or availability with respect to the content contained within.

Readers are encouraged to consult with appropriate professionals for advice and guidance related to their individual circumstances. The author and publisher disclaim any liability, loss, or risk, personal or otherwise, which is incurred as a consequence, directly or indirectly, of the use and application of any of the contents of this book.

The views and opinions expressed in this book are those of the author and do not necessarily reflect the official policy or position of any other individuals or organizations mentioned or referenced.

Every effort has been made to attribute and reference external sources and quotes appropriately. If any issues or concerns arise regarding the use of copyrighted material, please contact the author, and necessary corrections will be made in subsequent editions.

While the author has strived to make the book as accurate as possible, there may be unintentional errors or omissions. Please report any discrepancies to the author for future revisions.

Thank you for reading 'Unlock A Better Life: The Amazing Benefits of Living Your Life With Purpose.' Your support and understanding of this copyright and disclaimer are greatly appreciated.

6

About The Author

The author, Kristine J. Summers, is a kind and committed person who has made it her life's work to motivate constructive change in the world. She recognises the value of teaching her own family virtues like optimism, kindness, and empathy because she is a mother of three. Her work has been motivated by this insight.

Kristine is certain that these ideals have the potential to improve not only the lives of her own children but also society as a whole. Her writing and creation of content demonstrate her dedication to disseminating these values of kindness and optimism. She aspires to improve the lives of her readers and viewers through her work.

Kristine J. Summers's unique perspective as a loving mother adds depth and authenticity to her message. Her experiences in parenting and nurturing her children have shaped her belief in the transformative potential of kindness and empathy. She is a source of inspiration for those who seek to make the world a better place, one act of kindness and one positive message at a time.

Table Of Content

Table Of Content

Introduction

Are you ever stuck and wondering what God wants you to do with your life? Do you look around and wonder why others are living a life of purpose and you can't seem to get out of your own way? Do questions like "What makes me happy?", "How do I find my own happiness in life?", and "What makes a happy life?" ever crop up in your head? If you want to unlock your best life and truly find a purpose for living, then this book is for you!

Living your life with purpose has many amazing benefits. People with purpose have goals or beliefs that make their lives meaningful and worth living. Finding purpose in life is something that many people want, but it can be challenging to attain. You may have some preconceived ideas about the purpose of life that come from your family and the communities you grew up in. People sometimes misunderstand achievement as the purpose of life, but these types of achievements often don't bring the kind of fulfillment that comes with finding your personal sense of purpose.

Your personal sense of purpose guides and sustains you, giving you stability and a sense of direction. That's why finding purpose is essential for living a happy, healthy life. It can unlock greater satisfaction and success in all areas of your life. Behind every successful person is clarity of purpose, and unless you find yours, you'll continue to pass through life on auto-cruise.

Identifying, acknowledging, and honoring your purpose is the foundation to unlocking your best life. Knowing your purpose strengthens your sense of self; it gives you a way to explain who you are both to other people and to yourself.

This book aims to help you find your true self and do more of what you truly love.

Chapter One: What Are The Things That Makes You Happy In Your Life (Discover Your Passion)

Figuring out what brings you joy is a personal and ongoing journey. Happiness is not a place you can reach, but a state of being. It's not something you can find, but something you create. It's not something you should chase, but something you should embrace.

Happiness is here and now. It's in the small things that make you smile. It's in the people who love and support you. It's in the appreciation you feel for what you have. It's in the peace you find within yourself.

Passion is a powerful, almost uncontrollable emotion. It's a strong and intense feeling that drives someone to pursue a certain interest, hobby, activity, or goal with enthusiasm, dedication, and commitment. It's a deep and strong love for or interest in something, often surpassing mere preference. Passion can take many forms, such as a love for a certain hobby, a strong desire to excel in a certain career, or a strong commitment to a cause. It can give people a sense of purpose, fulfillment, and the motivation to overcome obstacles and challenges. Passion is usually characterized by a high level of energy, focus, and the willingness to invest a lot of time and effort into the object of one's passion.

It's a driving force that can lead to personal growth, creativity, and a sense of fulfillment.

Do you have anything in your life that you feel strongly about? Are you passionate about your job? Are you excited to go to work or do you dread it? What about the things you do outside of work? Do they keep you excited or are you just doing them to pass the time?

The more passion you have in your life, the happier you will be. Doing things you are passionate about motivates you to give it your all and do the best you can. Having passion for something increases your chances of success. Passion can bring you happiness in many ways:

1. Pursuing your passion gives you a sense of purpose and direction in life. Knowing what you love and are

enthusiastic about can provide a clear path and reason to set and achieve goals, leading to a greater sense of fulfillment and happiness.

2. Passion is often driven by intrinsic motivation, which means you engage in the activity for the sheer joy of it rather than external rewards. This intrinsic motivation can lead to a deep sense of satisfaction and happiness because you're doing what you love.

3. Engaging in your passion can lead to a state of flow, where you become fully absorbed in the activity, losing track of time and distractions. This flow state is associated with feelings of happiness and contentment.

4. Passion can give you the motivation and determination to overcome obstacles and setbacks. When you're passionate about something, you're more likely to persist in the face of challenges, which can lead to greater satisfaction and happiness when you achieve your goals.

5. Pursuing activities you're passionate about can trigger the release of feel-good chemicals in your brain, such as dopamine. These chemicals are associated with happiness and a sense of well-being.

6. Passion often allows you to express your authentic self. When you're engaged in something you're passionate about, you're more likely to be true to who you are, which can lead to greater self-acceptance and happiness.

7. Pursuing your passion can lead to continuous personal growth and development. The journey of improving your skills and knowledge in an area you love can be deeply fulfilling and contribute to your overall happiness.

8. Passion can also lead to the formation of social connections with like-minded individuals. Sharing your passion with others can foster a sense of community and belonging, which is linked to increased happiness.

It's important to remember that the connection between passion and happiness is strongest when your passion aligns with your individual values, interests, and abilities. Doing something you're passionate about and that brings you joy is more likely to lead to happiness than just following external expectations or doing something you're not truly enthusiastic about.

As you travel through life, keep your eyes and heart open to the opportunities that come your way. Nurture your curiosity and explore new experiences, even if your passion is still a mystery. With dedication and effort, you will eventually find your true calling. Remember, the journey of self-discovery is a winding one, but with perseverance and an open mind, you will eventually find your way.

Everyone's passions are unique, but there are some common themes that can help you explore your interests further. People can be passionate about a wide range of things, and these passions can bring joy in various ways.

Here are some common areas of passion and how they can bring happiness:

Sports, Fitness and Adventure: People who are passionate about health and fitness can lead to a healthier lifestyle and physical well-being. Achieving fitness goals and maintaining good health can bring happiness and a sense of vitality. This can include anything from participating in team sports to engaging in solo activities like running, cycling, or yoga. The benefits of such passions include improved health, stress relief, and a sense of camaraderie with fellow enthusiasts. Passion for adventure activities and extreme sports can lead to exhilaration and a sense of living life to the fullest. Overcoming physical and mental challenges can bring happiness.

Travel and Exploration: People who are passionate about exploring new places, cultures, and experiences can find incredible experiences and personal growth. Exploring new countries, cultures, and languages can broaden one's perspective and foster a greater appreciation for the diversity of the world. Travelling can broaden horizons, create memories, and provide a sense of adventure and happiness.

Volunteer Work and Philanthropy: Many people find purpose and passion in giving back to their communities and helping those in need. Engaging in volunteer work can provide a strong sense of purpose and happiness through helping others. The satisfaction derived from making a positive impact on others is often a driving force behind such passions.

Learning and Education: Passion for learning and acquiring knowledge can lead to personal growth and a sense of achievement. Education and intellectual pursuits can bring happiness through expanded understanding. Some individuals are deeply passionate about their own personal growth and self-improvement. This can manifest in a variety of ways, such as pursuing higher education, attending workshops and seminars, or simply reading and learning about a wide range of topics.

Creative Arts: Many individuals find their passion in expressing themselves through various creative outlets, such as acting, painting, writing, dancing, photography, or music. These pursuits allow them to communicate their emotions, ideas, and experiences, while also providing a sense of accomplishment and personal growth. It can provide an avenue for self-expression and a deep connection to one's inner self. Creating art can lead to happiness through the joy of expression.

Cooking and Food: For many people, their love for food extends beyond mere sustenance. Culinary enthusiasts find joy in experimenting with new recipes, exploring diverse cuisines, and sharing their creations with friends and family.

Relationships: Passionate love and strong emotional connections with family and friends can bring immense happiness. Nurturing these relationships can lead to a sense of belonging and support.

Technology and Innovation: With rapid advancements in technology, some individuals are passionate about staying on the cutting edge and exploring the latest gadgets, software, and innovations. This passion can lead to careers in fields such as software development, engineering, or design.

Causes and Activism: Passion for social or environmental causes can lead to a sense of purpose and the satisfaction of making a positive impact on the world. Being part of a larger movement for change can be emotionally rewarding. A growing number of people are becoming increasingly passionate about protecting the environment and promoting sustainable practices. This can involve advocating for policy changes, joining environmental groups, or adopting eco-friendly habits in their daily lives.

Hobbies and Interests: People can be passionate about hobbies like painting, playing musical instruments, gardening, cooking, or sports. These hobbies provide a creative outlet and a sense of accomplishment, leading to happiness.

Finding true happiness in life can be a challenge, but it's worth the effort. We all have different passions and interests, and it's important to explore these to discover what brings us joy and satisfaction.

It's also important to remember that happiness isn't always about material things; it can come from simple activities like journaling, meditating, and trying new things. It's also important to surround yourself with positive people who can help you stay motivated and inspired.

No matter what your passions and interests are, it's important to stay open-minded and curious about the world around you. With time and persistence, you can find your own unique passions and interests that bring you happiness. It's also important to remember that it's normal to experience negative emotions every now and then, but happiness can help us through tough times as well as the good.

Ultimately, it's important to know what makes you happy and to pursue it. Studies have shown that there is a positive correlation between well-being and happiness, and how happy you are can affect your life expectancy and health outcomes. So, take the time to figure out what brings you joy, excitement, satisfaction, and peace of mind, and make space for those things in your life. With the right attitude and effort, you can unlock your best life and experience lasting happiness.

What Can Make You Happy?

Gratitude: It's the little things in life that bring us joy and happiness. You don't need to make a long list, just take a few moments each day to think of something you're grateful for. You can express your gratitude in many ways, like writing it down in a journal, or simply saying it to yourself or someone you want to thank. Gratitude is a great way to increase your happiness and live a more fulfilling life. Consider keeping a gratitude journal or taking time to think about what you're thankful for each day.

Self-reflection is also important. Journaling can be a great tool to help you figure out what makes you happy. Write down moments when you felt genuinely happy and try to identify patterns or common elements. Journaling can help you explore your subconscious and resolve inner conflicts.

Mindfulness and meditation can also help you become more in tune with your emotions and thoughts. This can help you identify what truly brings you joy. Meditation is a great way to find out what makes you happy in life because it allows you to hear your inner voice more clearly. Mindfulness is a meditative practice that allows you to become aware of the present moment while cultivating compassion for yourself and others.

Doing a random act of kindness is another way to figure out what makes you happy. It doesn't have to be a grand gesture, even a simple smile or hello can make someone's day. Doing this regularly can help you realize how much happiness even a small act of kindness can bring.

Knowing your values is also important. Values are the things you cherish most in life and it's important to know what they are because they can help you figure out what it is that makes you happy. People whose values align with their personality have better self-esteem and are happier than those who don't know what their values are.

Experiment, discover, don't be afraid to experiment and try new things. You may discover new passions or interests you didn't know existed. Make a list of things to try and see what brings you true happiness.

Prioritize Relationships: Building and maintaining meaningful relationships with family and friends is essential for happiness. Studies have shown that social connection is one of the most important factors when it comes to feeling content. Strengthening your support network can be done by reaching out to family members you trust, surrounding yourself with optimistic people, making more friends, and spending time with people who support your dreams and goals.

Explore Your Passions: Doing activities that you genuinely enjoy can reduce stress and improve mental and physical health. Whether it's a hobby, sport, art, or volunteering, engaging in what you love can lead to increased happiness. Exercise has been shown to reduce stress, improve mood, and decrease symptoms of depression. Gardening and doing jigsaw puzzles can also bring joy.

Learn from Others: Talking to people who seem genuinely happy and content can offer valuable insights.

Volunteering: Helping others can give you a sense of purpose while also making a difference in your community. There are plenty of opportunities to give your time in service of causes that are important to you.

Set Goals: Establishing clear and achievable goals for different areas of your life can bring a sense of fulfillment and happiness.

Embrace Change: Understand that your sources of happiness may evolve over time. Be open to change and growth.

Take a break from technology and spend some time alone. This can help you get in touch with your inner self and gain clarity on what is important to you.

Animals have been bringing joy to people for a long time through their companionship, love, and loyalty. Studies have shown that having a pet can help improve mental health issues by providing a distraction from potentially harmful symptoms or experiences and helping owners meet other animal lovers. Additionally, interacting with a pet can cause the brain to release oxytocin, which is known as the "love hormone" and can lead to feelings of relaxation, positivity, and trust. Taking care of a pet can also encourage you to be more physically active.

If you are having difficulty understanding your happiness or facing mental health issues, consider talking to a therapist or counselor. They can provide guidance and support. Life is full of little moments of joy that can brighten your day.

Small Pleasures That Make Life Beautiful

There are many minor happiness increases in life that may make your day happier.

 Here are a few straightforward yet wonderful instances that might improve your mood and outlook on life:

1. Sunshine: On a clear day, experiencing the warmth of the sun on your skin.

2. Fresh Flowers: Fresh flowers may make you feel better just by looking at them and by smelling them.

3. Favorite Music: Your mood might quickly improve while you are listening to your favorite music.

4. A Good novel: Immersing yourself in an engrossing novel that takes you to a different place.

5. Random Acts of Kindness: Both doing and receiving random acts of kindness can lead to joyful experiences.

6. Pet Companionship: Spending time with and taking pleasure in the companionship of your favorite pets. Pet companionship is the practise of spending time with and appreciating the company of one's favorite pets.

7. Warm Beverages: Enjoying a soothing cup of tea, coffee, or hot chocolate.

8. Unexpected compliments: Being the recipient of a compliment or good words.

9. Playing games or being silly, or acting in a youthful manner that makes you grin.

10. Desserts and other sweet treats: Indulging in your preferred dessert or treat.

11. Cozy Moments: Putting on your coziest pyjamas or wrapping yourself in a warm blanket.

12. Trip Memories: Thinking back on previous trip experiences and recreating the memories.

13. Rainbows: After a rainstorm, spotting a rainbow in the sky.   14. Starry Nights: Admiring a night sky that is clear and full with stars.

15. Scented Candles: Light a scented candle to add a fragrant touch to your environment.

16. Random Acts of Kindness: Engaging in or seeing acts of generosity and compassion throughout the globe.

17. Walking about barefoot on the beach or on the grass.

18. Family Traditions: Participating in cherished family traditions or creating new ones.

19. Caring Conversations: Sincere exchanges with close friends and family that deepen your connections.

20. Early morning peace: Taking pleasure in the quiet and peaceful early morning hours.

21. A new-car smell

22. Grinning when dancing smiling when dancing

23. Singing in the shower while cleaning the wax out of your ears.

24. Getting a seat on a train, bus, or tube

25. Waking up before the alarm and realising there is still time to sleep.

26. Obtaining funds from unforeseen sources

27. Self-examination

28. Alone time

29. Laughing so hard it aches

30. Squeezing a spot

31. Cleaning the bathroom

32. A relaxing massage

33 The fresh sensation following a shower

34. Whenever your favourite song is played on the radio

35. Getting a deal during a sale

36. Hearing the rain or thunderstorms when indoors

37. The aroma of freshly-opened books or magazines

38. Being able to recall the name of something or someone you thought you'd forgotten

39. Having a newly made bed to sleep in

These brief moments of joy are all around us, and taking the time to notice them can result in a happier and more satisfying existence. Recognising and appreciating these little pleasures in the middle of our everyday routines is frequently the key to happiness.

Chapter Two: Finding Purpose And Meaning In Life

Finding purpose and meaning in life is a deeply personal journey, and it can look different for everyone. Purpose is having a clear and meaningful reason for existence or a specific goal or objective that drives an individual, while meaning is the deeper significance and interpretation of one's existence. Having a purpose often involves pursuing something that matters deeply to you, while meaning can be found in various ways, such as through relationships, personal accomplishments, spiritual or philosophical beliefs, contribution to society, or the understanding of one's role in the grand scheme of things.

Having a sense of purpose and meaning in life can bring a sense of fulfillment and overall well-being. It can also lead to increased optimism, resiliency, hope, joy, happiness, satisfaction, better physical health, a lower risk of death, being a more engaged student, enjoying the process of learning more, feeling a greater sense of belonging at school, increased career satisfaction, being a leader in the workplace, and higher income.

When it comes to having a sense of purpose, people can fall into one of four categories: the purposeful, the dreamers, the dabblers, and the disengaged. The purposeful have found something that is personally meaningful to them and that contributes to the greater good, while the dreamers think about and express great ideas but have not yet taken any practical action. The dabblers have engaged in potentially purposeful activities without committing to one in particular or sustaining their efforts over a long period of time, and the disengaged don't have a sense of purpose in life and don't have any desire or need to find one.

Work can be a great source of meaning, but it's important to have a sense of purpose that transcends work so we don't decompensate when our jobs shift, when we take leave, or when we retire. Individuals with a strong sense of purpose tend to live longer, have healthier hearts, and are more psychologically resilient. It also benefits organizations as employees with a strong sense of purpose work harder and stay longer.

Finding your purpose in life can bring a lot of psychological and emotional benefits and satisfaction. You want to feel more alive, more passionate, and more fulfilled. It's like uncovering a hidden masterpiece that's been waiting to be revealed. Your life's purpose is like a golden thread that can take the form of a career, a way of being, or an expression. It can be the driving force behind your life and help you feel connected to something larger.

But purpose isn't something that just happens to us. We can consciously cultivate it. It's not always easy to find, but it's worth the effort. When we wake up feeling lost, our sense of purpose can be the answer. It can be a sort of awakening or epiphany.
The importance of finding your purpose and how it can improve the quality of your life is immense.

Take some time to think about what made you want to know more about your life's purpose. What sparked joy in your life recently? These are simple starting points to help you find your purpose.Having a purpose makes life meaningful. It can lead to better relationships and improved physical health. Life without a clear purpose can be boring and unsatisfying. Once you find and understand your purpose, your life will never be the same again. You'll start attracting the things you've always wanted into your life.

Remember, everything starts from within. Your outer world is a reflection of your inner world. A purposeless life will always manifest fear, worry, and poverty. So, take some time to find and clarify your purpose and you'll be on your way to living a meaningful life.We all think we know ourselves, but only a few of us understand ourselves on a deeper level.

Knowing yourself can help you gain confidence and improve the quality of your life. You'll recognize your unique characteristics and hidden talents as you work towards your true purpose. In this process, you'll be aware of your strengths and weaknesses. By accepting yourself and doing your best to improve, you'll bring adventure and confidence into your life.

Your purpose will challenge you in a good way, as it often arises from a deep desire for a specific situation. You may find yourself questioning if your purpose can be achieved with the resources and skills you have right now. To make it happen, you'll need to develop or improve your skills and find the necessary resources. Reframing your limiting beliefs is the key to transforming your life, as your outer world reflects your inner world.

Finding purpose and meaning in life is an ongoing process, and it may change over time. Everyone's purpose is different, so it's important to stay open to exploration, be true to yourself, and continually seek and create meaning in your own unique way.To start realizing and living a more purpose-focused life, you can control your inner thoughts, find your passion, have a clear vision of life, define your priorities, and stay away from activities that make you feel drained and exhausted.

Learning to find your purpose in life is a lifelong journey, but once you've discovered it, you'll find that your life opens up in ways you never thought possible. You'll experience new depths of opportunity, and your eyes will be opened to all the possibilities around you. Finding your purpose is all about turning towards your thoughts and jumping in.

Finding your life's meaning doesn't have to be a difficult endeavor. Here are a few straightforward and detailed pointers to assist you on your trip.

You must first confront your internal conversation. You could encounter dread and resistance as you begin to examine your thoughts and goals. Your internal beliefs could try to hold you back by convincing you that you don't deserve to have a goal or that you'll never discover one. You need to be aware of it and bring it to people's attention if you want to stop it. It will be simpler to defeat these inner dragons if you are familiar with them.

You must also act to alter your internal dialogue if you want to learn how to find purpose in life.

Next, identify your area of greatest passion. Everyone looks forward to and wishes they could spend more time doing certain things. Your passion will assist you in determining what the meaning of life is. If you give these things your daily attention, you will be living your life intentionally and you will experience happiness all the time.

Then you create your golden thread. As you seek for your mission, let your creativity run wild. Don't be discouraged if you can't connect with someone straight away. Sleeping can occasionally be beneficial since it allows your subconscious to find a solution for you. Setting objectives the right method is quite beneficial as well.

Fourth, create a clear picture of the life you want. You may begin creating a vision for the life you want as you decide what your genuine priorities are. You will show up every day to work towards your biggest objective if you have faith that you can succeed.

Fifth, identify your genuine priorities and get rid of phony goals. While most people conduct their lives in accordance with others' expectations, you should live your life in accordance with your priorities. Determine your true priorities and the erroneous goals you are pursuing at the moment.

Determine what drains you lastly. Stop doing the activities that make you feel mentally or physically worn out. Your body and mind will suffer if you engage in pointless tasks, therefore delegate or stop doing them. Remember to run your own race, live your own life, focus on what matters to you, and build your life around your vision.

Finding purpose and meaning in life can be a challenge, but there are ways to invite a greater sense of purpose and meaning into your life.

1. To start, take time to reflect on your values, interests, and beliefs. What matters most to you? What activities or causes resonate with you on a deep level? Identifying your core values and setting personal goals that align with them can help you create a life that is both fulfilling and meaningful.

2. Explore your passions and interests. What activities or skills make you feel most alive and engaged? Consider how you can incorporate these into your life. Identifying your passions and interests is the first step, and then you can find ways to incorporate them into your daily life. Passion is often a key driver of purpose, as it connects us to our deepest desires and motivations. When we are engaged in activities that we are passionate about, we are more likely to feel a sense of fulfillment and purpose in our lives. By reflecting on your values and goals, and exploring your passions and interests, you can create a greater sense of purpose and meaning in your life. Incorporating your passions into your daily life can help you find greater joy and fulfillment, and discover new ways to contribute to the world around you.

.3. Set Goals: Identify objectives that are meaningful to you and that you can realistically achieve. Having goals to work towards can give you a sense of direction and purpose.

4. Help Others: Doing volunteer work and helping others can be a powerful way to find meaning. Acts of kindness and contribution often lead to a feeling of fulfillment.

5. Pursuing Personal Growth and Development: Keep learning and growing. Expanding your knowledge and skills can lead to a deeper sense of purpose.Pursuing personal growth and development is an essential part of living with intention and finding purpose and meaning in your life. By taking on challenges and opportunities for growth, learning new abilities, and exploring our interests, we can create a life that is fulfilling and rewarding, and develop a deeper sense of purpose and meaning.

i. Taking on challenges and opportunities for growth: Taking on challenges and opportunities for growth means being willing to step outside of our comfort zones and take on new experiences and challenges. This can include learning a new skill, taking on a new job, or pursuing a new hobby. By taking on these opportunities for growth, we can develop new strengths and abilities, and broaden our horizons in ways that can contribute to our overall sense of purpose and fulfillment.

ii. Learning new skills and exploring interests: Learning new skills and exploring our interests is another important aspect of personal growth and development. By increasing our knowledge and investigating new areas of interest, we can gain a greater sense of mastery and accomplishment, and discover new ways to express our unique talents and abilities. This can help us to feel more engaged and passionate about our lives, and contribute to a greater sense of purpose and meaning.

iii. How personal growth contributes to a sense of purpose: By taking on challenges, learning new skills, and exploring our interests, we can develop a greater sense of mastery and achievement, and discover new ways to contribute to the world around us. This can help us to feel more connected and involved in the world, and create a greater sense of purpose and meaning in our lives.

By taking on challenges, learning new skills, and exploring your interests, you can develop a greater sense of mastery and achievement, and discover new ways to contribute to the world around you.

6. Connect with Others: Establish strong, meaningful relationships with friends, family, and your community. Social connections can provide a sense of belonging and purpose.

Creating meaningful relationships is an important part of living with intention and finding purpose and meaning in your life.

Our relationships with others give us a sense of connection, support, and belonging, and can play a key role in our overall sense of fulfillment and purpose.

i. Nurturing relationships with others Nurturing relationships with others involves investing time and energy into building and maintaining meaningful connections with the people in our lives. This includes our family, friends, colleagues, and other members of our community. To nurture relationships, we need to be present, attentive, and supportive, and be willing to listen, communicate, and share our experiences with others.

ii. Surrounding yourself with supportive people: Surrounding yourself with supportive people is also an important aspect of building meaningful relationships. Supportive people are those who believe in us, encourage us, and help us to grow and develop as individuals. By surrounding ourselves with these types of people, we are more likely to feel supported, understood, and empowered to pursue our goals and dreams.

iii. How relationships contribute to a sense of purpose: Relationships give us a sense of connection and belonging, and can help us to feel that we are part of something greater than ourselves. By nurturing meaningful relationships and surrounding ourselves with supportive people, we can create a sense of community and purpose in our lives that is deeply fulfilling and rewarding.

Nurturing relationships with supportive people can help you feel more connected, loved, and valued, and contribute to a greater sense of purpose and meaning in your life.

Finding purpose and meaning in life is a journey that requires effort and self-reflection. To live with intention and discover a greater sense of purpose, we must reflect on our values and goals, explore our passions and interests, cultivate meaningful relationships, practice gratitude and mindfulness, and pursue personal growth and development.

It is important to remember that the journey towards purpose and meaning is ongoing, and requires a commitment to lifelong learning, growth, and self-discovery. We can start by embracing challenges and setbacks as opportunities for growth, and ensuring our actions align with our core values. We can also seek meaning in our work, explore spiritual and philosophical beliefs, engage in activities that lead to transcendent experiences, and plan for our legacy. Additionally, we can look to the people we admire for inspiration, and accept the imperfections of life.

By taking these steps, we can create a life that is rich, fulfilling, and deeply meaningful. Ultimately, by living with intention and striving towards a greater sense of purpose and meaning, we can create a life that is truly worth living.

48

Chapter Three: Overcome Your Fears And Phobias

Facing our fears and phobias is essential for living our best life, as they can limit our potential and affect our overall well-being. Fear is a natural and powerful emotion that is triggered when our brain perceives a potential danger. It is an important part of the human experience and serves as a protective mechanism.

When fear becomes excessive or irrational, it is known as a phobia. Phobias are a type of anxiety disorder and can cause significant distress and avoidance behavior. Unlike ordinary fears, which are often related to real dangers, phobias are characterized by their extreme and disproportionate nature. Phobias can have a major impact on our daily life, relationships, and overall well-being, as they often lead to avoidance behaviors that limit our activities and experiences.

Fear can be a real obstacle that holds us back from achieving our goals. It is our natural biological response when we are in the presence of actual or perceived danger, while a phobia is an overwhelming feeling of stress or anxiety about something, even when we are out of harm's way. A phobia usually triggers our fear response with a specific feared situation or object.

We don't have to let fear control us forever. There are several ways to overcome fears and phobias. If we have a phobia, we may realize that our fear is irrational, yet we still can't control our feelings. Just thinking about the feared object or situation may make us feel anxious. And when we are actually exposed to the thing we fear, the terror is automatic and overwhelming. We may go to great lengths to avoid it, even if it means inconveniencing ourselves or changing our lifestyle.

If we have a phobia, we can take steps to overcome it. With the right help and support, we can learn to manage our fears and phobias and live our best life.

Facing your fears can be a daunting task, but it is often the best way to deal with feelings of anxiety or excessive worry. One of the most effective ways to overcome your fears is to do the very thing that causes fear. This is known as 'exposure therapy', a psychological treatment that helps people confront their fears. It is important to remember that this does not mean putting yourself in dangerous situations, but rather learning to cope with irrational fears. Gradually, you can increase your exposure until you are able to tolerate the uncomfortable emotions associated with fear.

Conquering fear means learning to use it to your advantage. To do this, you must first find your center. This can be done through mindfulness meditation, which can help you gain clarity on what drives you. Once you have identified your fears, it is important to understand the root causes of them. This could be based on past experiences, childhood influences, or irrational thoughts. It is also important to recognize that fear can work to your advantage. When you use anxiety to your advantage, it can't ruin your life. In overcoming fear, it becomes your ally – a critical source of guidance to reach your full potential.

These are dependable tips to help you overcome your fears and phobias so you can live life to its fullest.

1. Identify your fears, understand their root causes, and recognize that fear can work to your advantage. With these steps, you can learn to use fear to your advantage and start living the life you want.

2. Educate Yourself:Sometimes, fear is caused by a lack of knowledge or misunderstanding. Take the time to learn more about the thing that you are afraid of. The more you know, the easier it will be to rationalize and demystify it.

3. Sit With Your Fear:It's important to know when to take action and when to take a step back and reflect. Acting too quickly to try and overcome your fear can lead to behaviors that do more harm than good, like drinking, overeating, or even repressing the feeling

entirely. The next time you feel fearful, try to do nothing. Take a few minutes to sit with your fear. Think about it. What is the root cause? Is it fear of the unknown? Fear of failure? What is the story you tell yourself about why you can't overcome this fear? Taking a moment to reflect can have a great effect on overcoming fear in a productive, deliberate, and effective way.

4. Gradual Exposure:Gradual exposure to your fears, also known as systematic desensitization, can be effective. Start with small, manageable steps to confront your fear, and gradually increase exposure over time.

5. Recognize The Excuses: Fear can make you put things off. "I'm really tired. I have other stuff to do. It's a dumb idea anyway." These excuses probably sound familiar, right? You've probably said them out loud and to yourself. Think about it. Is there any truth to these statements, or are you just making excuses to avoid potential failure? It's much easier and less painful to make excuses than it is to put in the effort it will take to work towards your goal, but excuses and opting out will

ultimately leave you feeling unfulfilled. If you want to conquer fear, you need to take a proactive approach. Recognize when you are using excuses and figure out how to overcome them. Too tired? Adjust your schedule so you can get a better night's sleep. Not enough time? Assess your priorities and find out where you can make time.

And the next time an excuse comes to you, make the decision to not give in to the little voice telling you "No," because it won't help you grow in the long run.

6. Cognitive Behavioral Therapy (CBT): CBT is a proven therapeutic approach for addressing fears and phobias. It helps you identify and change negative thought patterns and behaviors associated with your fears.

7. Adopt A Growth Mindset: When you're afraid, you tend to stay in one place. What if you make a mistake? What if you fail? You start to believe you can't progress at all, that you're incapable of it – the fear holds you back. One of the most powerful tips to overcome fear

and anxiety is to adopt a growth mindset. It's not about achieving your goals and being perfect every step of the way. No one is ever perfect all the time, so stop striving for that.

It's about getting comfortable with what you don't know and continuing anyway – this is the foundation of a growth mindset. "No matter how many mistakes you make or how slow your progress, you're still way ahead of everyone who isn't trying." As you work to overcome fear, you will realize that there will be lots of trials and tribulations along the way. As soon as you've accepted that the path to success includes growth and change, you'll be one step closer to attaining your goals.

8. Seek Professional Help: If your fears are having a significant impact on your daily life, consider seeking help from a therapist or counselor. They can provide guidance and structured treatments to address your specific fears.

9. Find Valuable Insight In Pain: No one likes pain. Most of us go to great lengths to avoid it. But pain can be a

great teacher. If you accept that your life and your efforts to achieve your goals will be painful at times, painful experiences become opportunities for growth.

When you let go of pain as a threat to your survival, it loses its power and becomes another tool for overcoming fear.

Everyone experiences hardships in life. It doesn't matter whether your setbacks are personal or professional – what matters are the lessons you take from those experiences and how you apply them to your future. Instead of letting a fear of uncertainty due to your past experiences dictate your decisions, actively choose to learn from those painful moments to be in control of your own life.

10. Mindfulness, Meditation, and Relaxation: Mindfulness, meditation, and relaxation exercises can be great tools to help manage anxiety and fear. They can help you to feel more in control and bring a sense of calm.

11. Visualize Your Success:Visualization techniques can be a great way to build confidence and reduce anxiety. Imagine yourself confronting and overcoming your fear. This can help you to feel more empowered.

You've done the mental work of figuring out why you're holding yourself back and what you need in life. But to really overcome fear, you need to practice these habits every day. Identify the problems, but focus your energy on solutions. Visualizing your goals is one of these solutions.

Visualizing your goals can help you to focus and direct your energy. It can take the form of priming, meditation, or imagery training. The important thing is that you see yourself succeeding and really immerse yourself in your goal. This will help to condition your brain to believe that anything is possible, which is a key step in overcoming fear.

12. Positive Affirmations: Use positive affirmations to challenge negative thoughts related to your fears. Replace them with more positive and rational beliefs.

13. Accept That You'll Fail: One of the biggest fears people have when it comes to achieving their goals is that they'll fail. But failure can be a great teacher. If you accept that failure is part of success, you'll be less afraid of it. Failure can provide you with valuable learning experiences that will help you in the future. Everyone fails, even successful people.

Our society tends to focus on successes and not failures, which can give the false impression that you must never fail to be successful. But part of overcoming fear is recognizing that everyone has encountered failure on their path to greatness.

The sooner you realize that your fear of failure is preventing you from achieving your dreams, the sooner you'll be able to accept the possibility of failing and move on.

14. Get Support: Share your fears with trusted friends or family members. Having a support system can provide emotional reassurance and encouragement. It's great to have a group of people encouraging you and giving helpful tips. You'll feel more calm and supported when

your friends are around to help you out and tell you what you did well.

Fear can be a powerful force that can keep us from living our best lives. It can be paralyzing and prevent us from taking risks and achieving our goals. But it doesn't have to be that way. We can learn to recognize our fear responses and use them to our advantage.

People who are living a life of purpose have also experienced fear, but they have the courage to take action despite it. They understand that the only way to build confidence is to take action even when fear is present.

The key to overcoming fear is to set realistic goals and be patient and persistent in your efforts. Self-care is also essential to maintain good mental and emotional health. Keeping a fear journal can help you track your progress and document your experiences, thoughts, and feelings related to your fears.

Surrounding yourself with successful people can also help you stay motivated and focused on your goals.

When you have people who you look up to and who will hold you accountable, it can help you stay on track and overcome fear. Finally, don't forget to celebrate your achievements, no matter how small. Recognizing your progress can be a great source of motivation.

Chapter Four: The Amazing Benefits Of Living With Purpose

A growing body of studies suggests that the answer to the question

"Do you have a purpose in life?" may hold the secret to your wellbeing and happiness.

What exactly is "purpose in life,"? Though, simply expressed, "purpose" can refer to the conviction that your actions are morally righteous. When you believe that you are acting in accordance with your values and aspirations, you have a feeling of purpose. You can benefit from a crop of advantages regardless of your goal. Your physical, mental, and emotional well-being may all be enhanced by having a purpose in life.

"Purpose" offers a variety of other benefits as well, including better sleep. A sense that your activities are worthwhile could be a key to healthy aging. Living with purpose is knowing that your life has meaning, value, and importance, even when the day-to-day grind gets to you. It means that through doing meaningful work, your contribution and your life make a positive impact on the lives of others.

Having purpose means that what you do serves humanity positively. Living for a purpose will make you happier, more content, more successful, more graceful, more resilient through hard times, more excited, and more alive!

Living with purpose can bring about a wide range of amazing benefits, enhancing your overall well-being and quality of life.

Here are some of the significant advantages of living with purpose:

1. Fulfillment: Living a purpose-driven life often leads to a deep sense of fulfillment and satisfaction. Knowing that your actions have meaning and make a

difference can bring joy and contentment. The key to overcoming depression and sadness is realizing that someone's life is improved because you exist.

The most undeniable way to feel happy is by connecting with a strong sense of purpose and contribution. If you're looking to feel happier—and I think we all are—adding more purpose to your life can put you on the fast track to fulfillment. Because nothing will give you more joy than knowing that your life has meaning, purpose, and value.

Nothing will fill you up with more pride, joy, and contentment than knowing that you're adding something valuable and important to the world, to humanity, and to the universe. That strong correlation between purpose and happiness makes perfect sense.

Depression, dark moods, and sadness usually originate from feeling like a lost soul, feeling out of control, feeling like you have no direction, and feeling like your life has no purpose. Nothing feels worse or more depressing than that confusion, frustration, and disappointment of feeling like your life is headed in a bad direction or no direction at all.

Because when you don't have a powerful "Why" that drives you or a sense of contribution to the world, it's easy to throw your life away into negative habits, negative jobs, negative relationships, and negative behavior. When you don't have a powerful purpose, that's driving you, it's easy to just throw in the towel on life.

Knowing that your life has purpose, direction, meaning, and value can give you a reason to get out of bed every day, a reason to live, and a reason to feel happy on a daily basis. Living with purpose will give you all the fulfillment you'll ever need.

2. Personal Growth: Pursuing your purpose often involves continuous learning and growth, which can lead to a more enriched and meaningful life.

3. Direction, Guidance, and Comfort Through Hard Times: Hard times are a reality that we all have to face at different points in our lives. We all struggle through dark moments, situations, failures, obstacles, trials, and tribulations.

We all have periods of time when we try our best to our best to succeed, but we fail anyway. And we all pass through moments when we try our hardest to make things right, but they still go wrong, anyway. The hard times are unavoidable. You can't escape the struggle. But what you can do is use your purpose to comfort, guide, and support you through the storms. Because when everything falls apart, the purpose will be the support system that helps you piece your life back together.

Knowing that there are people out there depending on you to make it through will motivate you to keep faith alive, keep persisting, and keep persevering until you find your break in the clouds.

Having a clear purpose provides you with a sense of direction in life. It helps you set goals and make decisions that align with your values and passions.

Knowing that your life has value will push you toward resilience, healing, and recovery from your trauma. Your purpose will be the shining light that will guide

4. Positive Self-Esteem: Living with purpose can boost self-esteem and self-worth. You feel more confident in your abilities and the impact you make on the world.

5. Endless Motivation: A strong sense of purpose can be a powerful motivator. It gives you the drive and determination to pursue your goals, even in the face of challenges. Nothing can motivate you more than having a positive effect on other people.

Money, fame, power, and advancement all come secondary to the most powerful source of motivation in the world: Purpose.

Every successful person has a Why that motivates them to get up every morning, go out into the world, and do what they do. Every successful person has a reason, a Why, and a purpose behind their achievement.

Accomplished people always attach their work to a cause that's bigger than themselves. That purpose becomes the driving force that makes those people successful. Purpose is the purest form of motivation there is.

Knowing that you have people out there depending on you—mouths to feed, customers to serve, fans to please, and followers to inspire—makes giving up impossible.

Because when you realize that your work has a positive effect on others—when you know that the lives of others will be worse off if you throw in the towel—something will always motivate you to do whatever it takes to be successful

6. Resilience: People with a strong sense of purpose tend to be more resilient. They can better navigate adversity and bounce back from setbacks.

7. Improved Mental Health: Purpose is linked to lower rates of depression and anxiety. It provides a positive focus and can help reduce stress and negative emotions.

8. Longevity: Studies have shown that individuals with a strong sense of purpose tend to live longer and have a higher quality of life in their later years, that individuals with stronger purpose in life had lower all-cause mortality. Having a purpose also decreased the chance of premature death.

9. Physical Health: Some research suggests that living with purpose may be associated with better physical health. It can lead to healthier lifestyle choices and habits.

10. Stronger Personal Relationships: Having a sense of purpose can improve your relationships. It often leads to more meaningful connections and a greater sense of empathy and compassion. Higher ratings for the belief that life is worthwhile were correlated to the likelihood of having a life partner, less risk of divorce, more contact with friends, membership in various organizations,

volunteering, and a greater number of close relationships. People with strong purpose in life also experienced less loneliness.

11. Contribution to Society: A sense of purpose often involves contributing positively to your community or the world. This can create a legacy and impact that extends beyond your own life.

12. Happiness: People who live with purpose tend to report higher levels of happiness and life satisfaction. Knowing that you're making a difference and living authentically can be a source of joy. "Happiness" included a range of positive feelings from pleasure to life satisfaction to the sense of contribution to a larger purpose.

13. Emotional Well-Being: A purpose-driven life can lead to better emotional well-being, including increased positive emotions and a sense of contentment.

14. Energy and Vitality: Pursuing your purpose can provide you with a renewed sense of energy and vitality. It can make you feel more alive and engaged with life.

Purpose not only gives you fulfillment, guidance through hard times, and motivation to win, it can also give you a powerful and rare feeling of aliveness. Purpose makes you come alive.

Having a sense of purpose, meaning, value and contribution to humanity gives you that certain spark, aliveness, excitement, and passion for life that makes successful people so attractive to the world.

Doing meaningful work can transform you from dragging yourself through your 9-to-5 to love every single second of your day.

Without purpose, life can feel really boring, and a routine. But when you find your Why, life becomes like a great adventure. And every day that you do your work is another important step in your journey.

Purpose makes you feel happy, grateful, excited to be alive, and lucky to be who you are. It's a rare and powerful sense of aliveness that purposeful people enjoy on a daily basis. So if you do know what your purpose is, congratulations on connecting with your Why.

Having a stronger sense of purpose can mitigate the negative effects of the stress hormone cortisol. The presence of purpose can counteract stress, improving the immune system, calming the heart rate, and reducing blood sugar levels.

And, as you travel along the road to your purpose, you'll begin to understand how failure and mistakes are all part of the road trip! No one is perfect, and no journey in life can be without the occasional hiccups and setbacks. But you don't need to worry about these. As your inner drive to achieve your purpose will overcome all difficulties that you face.

To boost your sense of accomplishment, celebrate each small goal you achieve on the way to the big one.

71

So now you know some of the great benefits of pursuing a purpose, and I hope you feel inspired to find and follow yours.

Chapter Five: Be Yourself, Live Your Best Life

Living your best life is all about taking control of your life and your thoughts and doing everything you can to live the life you want. It's about taking risks, embracing your passions, and living each day to the fullest. You must know yourself better, embrace your true self, and stay true to your values and passions. It's about expressing your true self in a world that pressures us to conform. It's about finding purpose and meaning, pursuing your passions, and positively impacting the world.

To live your best life, you have to take life by the horns and make a difference. You have to find your meaning in life and work hard to live it to the fullest. You have to believe in yourself and follow your dreams. You have to adopt a "you can do it" attitude and force yourself to chase and follow your dreams. Happiness will not always be a motivator, but think about how you would

73

feel if you woke up every day looking forward to it. It's entirely up to you to live your best life.

Below are subtle actions you can take to live your life to the fullest, being yourself and living your best life.

It's Entirely Up To You: The sooner you realize only you can do this, the better. No one can help you live the best life, happiness comes from within. Even if you find people that uplift your life, your happiness and your drive and commitment has to come from inside. You have to adopt a you can do it attitude and force yourself to chase and follow your dreams in life. You have to find your meaning and your purpose in life and carve a future for yourself. You might not have any idea on what this is, but if you dig deep enough. You will find that doing things that make you happy is a great place to start.

Happiness will not always be a motivator but think about how you would feel if you woke up everyday looking forward to it.

Better yourself: Look at your life carefully with lessons learned in mind.   What have you done that has had a massive impact on yours, other people's or your work life? What have you done that has made you feel like you have accomplished great things? Anything that has put a smile on your face. Looking inside yourself will help you to become a better person by realizing what makes you tick, what makes you smile.

What does your best life look like: What is it that would make your life complete? If you close your eyes and manifest your dreams, what do you see? Can you clearly see what life would look like? If not then practice this everyday, what would make you happy, what would make you complete? What would get you out of bed with a smile on your face. Seeing and smelling what you want in life will start the process for attracting these things into your life.

Make a plan to start your best life: Once you can see it and you know what you want and it has to be what you want and not what you do not want. This is a very important part of the process as the Universe has a habit of attracting negative things into your life too. So this is about staying positive with your thoughts and not thinking negatively. Even if you have no clue how you are going to do this then just write down what you want. When you start the process of thinking about how to get it, you will find that the answer comes right into your mind in a moment of clarity.

Stop all doubts: Your dreams and your best life might seem like you will never get there. It might seem so big that you scare yourself thinking I can't do this. Well you can and you can do anything and most of it starts with not overthinking things in the first place. This takes time to train your mind but any excuses that come up or negative associations you just have to keep telling yourself that you can do it, you can do it. Don't let those silly thoughts put you off, just keep moving forward and chase your dreams.

Don't be jealous of others: Jealousy is a horrible emotion and you shouldn't ever let it into your thoughts. Whenever you feel jealous about something you need to stay calm and think things through properly before reacting to the situation. You need to learn how to be nice in these situations instead.

Stay Consistent: You will struggle with knockbacks and failures and the overthinking process. So it is really important that you learn how to stay consistent with your positive thoughts. Keep striving forward, see every knockback and failure as a step closer to getting what you want. Don't take things personally, all of us fail it is a natural process. All of us get rejected when you can see this as a positive in life and just a challenge to overcome. Your best life will start to appear before you know it. Become invincible and keep getting back up after every knockdown.

Be kind to yourself: Empathy is important and you will have to be kind to yourself through this process as well. Well do not beat yourself up about things. If you want to live the best life then there are going to be hurdles and you will make mistakes. You cannot look back on everything and beat yourself up, all you have to do is learn from your mistakes and don't make the same mistake twice. But just be kind to yourself and yes you could have done better and next time you will because you would have learnt your lesson.

Live your life: Life really is what you make of it everyday. When you realize that you control your thoughts in life then you put yourself in a very powerful position. You stop blaming others on your moods, situations that happen. You take control of your own destiny and make other people's opinions obsolete. So you choose to be happy, you choose to be kind, choose to work hard, you choose to change jobs, you choose to change houses. In fact everything in your life is your choice the hard thing is making those choices, standing by them and working hard to chase your dreams and make them happen.

Don't let others put you down: The amount of time I see people quit things because other people have ridiculed them and ultimately put them off living their best life. This is not fair, no one should control your thoughts and feelings like this. Everyone in your life should add value to it, they should encourage you, nurture you, big you up and help you get there. There is enough room on this planet for everyone to succeed. So if you find people in your life that make you feel like crap then do not listen to them and preferably get rid of them as quickly as possible and surround yourself with awesome people instead.

Don't let the past obscure your future: If you have had a bad experience in the past do not let this get in the way of living your life moving forward. Everything that happens is for a reason and the likelihood of it happening again is probably not going to happen. You have to think about the laws of the universe being real here and that attracts like.

Habits: Everything you do is a habit and it takes 2 months to form good habits once you are in a routine. So all the above you have to do for a minimum of 2 months before you will routinely start to get up smiling and follow your dreams. So don't give up early, keep staying positive.

Get out there and do it: Go and chase your dreams, you owe it to yourself to get the motivation to do this. You can do anything you want to in life, I'll say it again, you can do it. There is absolutely nothing stopping you from living your best life apart from you and your thoughts. Believe you can do this and you will.

If you want to live your best life, there are some practical tips and tools you can use to get there.

Firstly, be the best version of yourself. Don't try to be someone else or what other people want you to be. Focus on who you want to be and be proud of what makes you unique.

Secondly, observe yourself. Notice how you respond to different situations, your habits, what makes you happy, what frustrates you, how you behave under pressure, and what gives you energy and what drains you. Spend a week writing down your observations.

Thirdly, identify your bad habits. Notice the things that don't make you feel good and do more of the things that make you happy and give you energy. Work on reducing and eliminating the habits that waste your time and energy. Fourthly, set intentions. Decide what living the best life looks like for you and be intentional about it. Setting intentions is different from setting goals. Goals are the things you want to achieve, while intentions are the positive feelings and emotions you are seeking.

Lastly, visualize living your best life. Choose a specific intention and how you will feel once it is accomplished and take the time to daydream and allow your imagination to wander.

Now that you have a clear vision of what your ideal life looks like, let's look at some practical steps you can take to make it a reality.

1. Focus: Whatever you do, focus on it. Don't try to do multiple things at once, as it's impossible to do them all well. Focused work is the most productive and least tiring.

2. Take Responsibility for Taking Action: Taking action can be intimidating, as we fear both failure and success. It can be easy to feel too busy to make progress, but it's up to you to take action and make your best life a reality.

3. Live in the Present: Every day is a new opportunity to live your best life. Don't wait for the perfect moment to start, as it will never come. Use what you have now and take action. Fancy gadgets, better clothes, or a slimmer body won't make you better - only action will.

4. Practice Mindfulness: Research has shown that mindfulness can lead to greater happiness and better physical and mental health. Mindfulness is the ability to observe the present moment without judgement. To practice it, take a deep breath and notice how it feels as it goes into your lungs. How does your body feel? Are your muscles stiff or relaxed? Do you feel warm or cold? Use your five senses to describe your immediate experience.

5. Declutter: This applies to both your physical environment and the people you spend time with. Ask yourself if something or someone brings you joy. If the answer is yes, keep it. If you hesitate or say no, donate or discard it.

6. Relish the Simple Things: When we're busy, it's easy to forget to appreciate what we have. Take time to focus on the small things and be grateful for them. Gratitude is strongly linked to greater happiness, so be thankful for what you do have, rather than resentful of what you don't.

7. Journaling is a great way to get your thoughts in order and manage stress and anxiety. Writing down your thoughts and feelings can help ease symptoms of depression, too. It's easy to get overwhelmed by life, but journaling can help you productively cope.

8. Learning is a great motivator, so why not make a bucket list of things you'd like to do and learn? It could be anything from reading up on a particular topic to traveling to a new place.

9. Making someone's day doesn't have to be a big gesture. Even small, thoughtful things like offering a genuine compliment or opening the door can make a big difference.

10. Taking care of your body is important, too. Eat natural, unprocessed foods and drink plenty of water. Exercise should be something you enjoy, not something you have to do. Try out different activities like walking the dog, gardening, yoga, swimming, or dancing.

11. We all have an inner critic that tells us we're not good enough. The next time it appears, acknowledge it and list all the reasons it's wrong.

12. Living your best life doesn't always go according to plan. Be prepared to change the plan as life throws things at you.

13. Flow is a great way to connect with your true self and experience positive emotions. Find activities that put you in a flow state and you'll be on your way to living your best life.

14. Make a Commitment to Your Goals: Having a strong sense of community is essential for our overall happiness and wellbeing. If you're feeling disconnected or want to build a stronger sense of belonging, try reaching out to a different friend each day, joining a spiritual group, support group, or book club, or attending cultural or community events that align with your interests. To stay connected with your favorite friends, why not plan a

weekly hike, coffee hour, Zoom call, happy hour, or email/text check-in?

Remember, you get what you give. Show up when people you care about need help or want to connect. Set healthy boundaries with people who drain your energy.

15. Get Moving: Exercise is a key factor in staying healthy and happy and reaching our full potential. Studies have shown that exercise can help prevent depression, reduce long-term illness, boost our moods, and increase our lifespan. It's not just exercise that matters, though; how we move our bodies throughout the day, even when we're sitting at our desks, can make a difference.

Recent research has shown that simply sitting up straight can lead to more positive thoughts about ourselves and our lives.

16. Spend Time in Nature: One of the best ways to live our best lives is to spend time in nature. From the vitamin D we get from the sun to the sense of connection to something greater, the benefits of nature are

undeniable. We now know how important it is to protect our natural spaces, parks, and trees, not just for our enjoyment, but also for our physical and mental health.

Finally don't forget to hit the reset button often. Take a minute to refocus and reset your energy. Stretching, taking a deep breath, and setting goals or intentions can help. Knowing how to reset is important for personal growth.

At the end of the day, life is short, so make the most of it. You can't control all the bad things that happen, but you can change your attitude towards them and create your best life.

Here are some simple ways to do just that:

Live each day with a fresh start.

Don't let the past hold you back.

Be true to yourself.

Don't try to be someone else.

Stop complaining and start taking action.

Focus on what you want before you think about how to get it.

Create your own opportunities.

Live consciously each day.

Don't just coast through life.

Be dedicated to your development. Take classes.

Reflect on yourself. Utilize your talents.

Don't just stick to what you know, but focus on what will help you grow the most.

Know yourself:

This means understanding who you are and what you stand for. Be aware of your identity.

Find your life purpose:

Set the mission statement for your life, one that will motivate you to live your life to the fullest. Live in accordance with your purpose. What can you start doing right away that will let you live 100% in line with your purpose? How can you stay true to your purpose in every situation you are in, every second of the day?

Set your life commandments:

Define your personal commandments to live your best life. What sayings and principles do you want to follow in your life?

Recognize your values:

Values are the core of what makes you, you. Hold yourself to the highest standard.

Every one of us has our own set of ethics and principles. Live up to them every day. Also, live in full alignment with your purpose, commandments, and values.

Stop postponing life:

Are you putting any parts of your life on hold? What is one area of your life you have been delaying, avoiding, or denying? Uncover that and start working on it.

Create your life handbook:

Your life handbook is your guide to living your best life. It contains your mission statement, values, goals, personal strengths, blind spots, and action plans. Start with a few basic pages, and then build on them.

Design your ideal life:

What is your ideal life? Design it. Firstly, assess your life via the life wheel. Then, ask yourself what it takes to live a 10/10 life. What is the life that will make you shout for joy? There are no limits in life — only those you set for yourself!

Set your goals:

After you design your ideal life, set your 5-year, 3-year, and 1-year goals. The more specific they are, the better!

Take action on your goals and dreams:

Create an action plan for your goals and work on it! Make your bucket list, which is a list of things to do before you die. Then, get out there to accomplish them. Don't do things just for the sake of doing them. Always evaluate what you're doing and only do it if there is meaning behind it.

Don't be scared to quit the things that don't serve your path.

Do the things you love because life is too precious to be doing anything else. If you don't enjoy something, then don't do it. Spend your time and energy on things that bring you fulfillment and joy.

Discover your passion in life:
What sets you on fire? Go out there to find out what you love to do.

Turn your passion into a full-time career:
Then, start pursuing it. Stop working in a job you feel passionless about. Quit your job when you are ready to do it full-time.

Turn your passion into a huge success:
Turn your passion into a multi-million dollar business. Better yet, make it a multi-billion dollar one.

Learn from criticism:
Be open to criticism but don't be affected by it. Criticism is meant to help you be a better person. Learn from it.

Be positive:

Is the glass half empty or half full? What if I say it's neither? It's actually all full — the bottom half is water and the top half is air. It's all a matter of perception. Take on perspectives that empower you, not those that bind you. If you can see the positive side of everything, you'll be able to live a much richer life than others.

Don't talk badly about other people:

 If there's something you don't like about someone, say it to his/her face — otherwise, don't say it at all. It's not nice to badmouth others, and it also reflects a small mind.

Be understanding:

If everyone only sees life from his/her perspective, we'll forever be close-minded and insular. See things from others' points of view.

Be kind:

Show compassion and kindness to everyone around you.

Develop 100% self-belief:

Believe in yourself and your abilities. Identify your limiting beliefs and replace them with empowering ones. If you don't believe in yourself, how can you expect others to believe in you?

Let go of the past and all the negative emotions that come with it. Forgive those who have wronged you in the past, and don't get too attached to material possessions or status. Instead, focus on living life to the fullest. Cut ties with people who don't serve you and spend more time with those who do. Build genuine connections with those around you, and don't be afraid to reach out to old friends.

Do something kind for someone every day, and help those in need. If you're single, go out and date, and if you're not, make deeper connections with your partner.

Take time to review your life and set goals, and make sure to overcome procrastination. Spend at least 30 minutes a day working on something that will bring you fulfillment and happiness.

Make new friends, and declutter your life. Keep learning and developing yourself, and write a letter to your future self.

Keep improving yourself. Equip yourself with a vast amount of knowledge. While you can usually only reach level 99 in video games, in real life you can level up to infinity. If necessary, pursue further studies.

Develop your skills. Level up. Spend more than 10,000 hours honing each skill. Try something new. What is something you would normally not do? Step out of your comfort zone and try something different. It could be something small like taking a different bus route, trying a new food item, or picking up a new hobby. Or it could be something bigger like studying a different field, learning a new skill, or traveling to a place you've never been before. There are no limits (as long as it's not illegal or morally wrong, of course)!

Get out there.

(i) Get out there geographically. Go out, travel, and explore the world. Go on a sailing trip. Go backpacking by yourself and visit as many countries as you can. Take a road trip and visit all the places you see.

(ii) Get out there situationally. Stop sticking to routines and comfort zones. Try something different.

(iii) Get out there in life. Stop watching TV and living vicariously through the TV characters. Go and live the life of your dreams.

Be the best at what you do. Aim for the 1st position in what you do. If you're going to spend your time doing something, you might as well be the best at it!

Don't settle. Don't settle for less. Don't settle for someone you don't like as your partner. Don't settle for a job you don't like. Don't settle for friends who make you feel like a lesser person. Don't settle for a weight you are unhappy with. Go for what you really want.

Push yourself. What are you doing now? How can you achieve more? Set bigger goals. Explore your limits and break them.

Embrace new ideas. Don't mentally limit yourself. Let your mind be a breeding ground for new ideas.

Create your inspirational haven. Transform your room into a place you love. Do the same for your work desk. Get rid of things that make you unproductive. Surround it with things that inspire you and motivate you into action.

Act as your ideal self would. All of us have an ideal vision of who we want to be. What is your ideal self like? How can you start to be your ideal self now?

Set your role models in life. With role models, you become much better than you can be by yourself. Seeing them and what they do reminds you of what you can be and what you can do, so they drive you to greater heights.

Get mentors/coaches. There's no faster way to improve than to have someone work with you on your goals. Not only will they push you to achieve more, but they'll also share important advice which you can use to create even more success for yourself. Many of my clients approach me to coach them and the result is this: they make significantly more progress and get better results than if they had worked alone.

Uncover your blind spots. The more you uncover, the more you grow, and the better you become.

Increase your consciousness. Having a high consciousness level means being able to transcend beyond fear-based reactions and make wise choices that positively impact everyone.

Ask for feedback. As much as we can try to uncover our blind spots, there will be blind spots that we cannot identify. Asking for feedback gives us an added perspective about ourselves. Some people to approach are our friends, family, colleagues, boss, and even acquaintances.

Generate passive income. Create passive income streams so that your income is not tied to the time you spend on work. Of course, you'll continue to work, but only because you want to and not because you have to.

Help others live their best lives. There is no better way to grow than to help others grow. Ultimately, the world is one. We are all on this journey of life together.

Get married / Start your family / Have kids!

Improve the world. Many things in the world need your help and attention. Poverty. Disaster recovery. Illiteracy. Children in need. Depleting rainforests. Animal rescue. Endangered species. How can you do your part?

Be clear about your end goal. What is it that you are striving for? Is the task you are working on bringing you closer to that goal? If not, set it aside. As long as you keep working on tasks that are aligned with your end goal, you will eventually reach it.

For each goal you have, there are different paths to achieve it. Pick the most effective path that will bring you to your goal with the least amount of effort.

Prioritize. As you embark on the path for your goals, focus on the important tasks and cut out the less important ones. Work on the 20% actions that give you the 80% results.

Live in the moment. Do you often find yourself with a busy mind? Take a step back and be present. The only time you are ever living is in this moment. Meditation can help clear your mind.

Appreciate the little moments. Snuggling under warm covers on a rainy day. Having ice cream on a hot day. A kiss with your loved one. Being with your best friend. A walk by the park. The breeze on your face.

Quiet, alone time. Watching the sunrise/set. Enjoy all these little moments of life. They are what make up your life.

Take a break. Being the best also requires you to take breaks when needed. Make sure you rest when needed. Doing so will help you stay on the long road ahead.

Stop wanting things a certain way. There are downsides to perfectionism and how to overcome them. Be firm on your end goals and ideals, but let go of the obsession to have things done a certain way. You'll realize that when you do so, you achieve what you want.

Focus on creation. Think about what you can bring to the world and create that.

Don't criticize or judge others. Respect others for who they are.

The only person you can change is yourself. Stop expecting others to behave in a certain way. Rather than demand that others around you change, focus on changing yourself. You'll be happier and live a more fulfilling life this way.

Practice gratitude. Be grateful for everything you have today, and everything you will get in the future.

Express gratitude. Let the people who've touched you know about your gratitude towards them. You'll be surprised what a little act like this can do. If you don't tell them, they'll never know.

Let loose and have fun. Sing at the top of your lungs. Dance in the rain. Run barefoot and feel the ground underneath your feet. Hug everyone you know. Release yourself of your self-imposed shackles and be free!

Get into nature. Many of us live in concrete jungles. Get out of the urban city environment and soak in the beauty of nature.

You have a choice. Recognize you always have a choice in how to live your life.

Laugh more. Are you reading this with a straight face? Smile and have fun.

Embrace change. The only thing that's constant is change. Change means growth. Rather than resist change, learn to be versatile so you can make the best out of the changes that come. In fact, become an agent of change.

Be more risk inclined. Don't be afraid to take risks. The bigger your risks, the bigger your return.

Embrace mistakes. The more mistakes you make, the more experienced you become, and the higher your chances of success. Make sure to identify lessons from each experience so that you can build on them.

Embrace disappointments. Many people try to avoid feeling disappointed. They develop a negative relationship with disappointment. However, disappointment is part and parcel of being human — it reflects your real emotions. Don't resist it — instead, embrace it. Learn to channel your disappointment and turn it into positive energy.

Be your best self. When we work on being better people, we live a richer life.

Love yourself. You are the one constant in your life. Remember to always treasure and love yourself. You deserve nothing less.

Love others. Be grateful to all the people around you because they help you grow. They enrich your life experience. Without them, your life would not be the same.

Finally, Love life. Living is a fascinating experience. How we're all on earth with millions of species, 30,000 different life forms, and over 7 billion people, and everyone is thriving in their own way, existing, co-existing, and co-creating. There's so much we don't know out there and so much to be experienced that it's just wonderful. As you live on earth, remember to love life. It's the only way to live.

Please do not waste your life and throw it away, do everything you can to make your life enjoyable and the others around you. Spread love and give kindness, look for opportunities in life because you owe it to yourself.

Live each day like it counts, and remember, it's your choice. Your best life is unique to you. Don't compare yourself to others – focus on living your best life, and enjoy the learning, exploration, and experiences along the way.

Conclusion

At the core of human existence lies a fundamental desire to find purpose and meaning in our lives. We yearn to know that our lives have significance, and that we are making a difference in the world. Yet, the search for meaning can often seem elusive and overwhelming, especially in a world that can sometimes feel chaotic and uncertain. The pursuit of meaning is not only a personal goal, but an essential aspect of our well-being. In conclusion, "Unlock A Better Life: The Amazing Benefits of Living Your Life With Purpose" beautifully illustrates the transformative power of embracing purpose in our lives. Throughout these pages, we've journeyed through the profound impact that purpose can have on our well-being, relationships, and overall sense of fulfillment. We've seen that a life guided by purpose is a life filled with passion, resilience, and a sense of direction.

This book has shown us that purpose is not a luxury but a necessity, offering a roadmap to a life brimming with meaning and significance. By exploring the stories, experiences, and research presented within these pages, we've come to understand that purpose is the key to unlocking our true potential. Some people refer to a life purpose as a 'calling'. But, whatever you choose to name it, your purpose should contribute positively to society in some way, while at the same time bringing satisfaction and a sense of achievement to yourself. Your purpose will also provide meaning to your life. And, this will give you the mental tools you need to face the ups and downs in life that you'll inevitably encounter on the way to reaching your goals. When you're able to find meaning and purpose in your life, your fears will dissipate. That's the power of knowing where you're going and what you're aiming for.

As we close this chapter, let us carry with us the knowledge that living with purpose isn't just an abstract concept; it is a practical and tangible pathway to living a richer, more fulfilling life. With purpose as our guiding star, we can transcend obstacles, find joy in the journey, and ultimately unlock the doors to a better life that awaits us all. So, may this book inspire you to embark on your own purpose-driven adventure, and in doing so, may you discover the amazing benefits of living your life with true and unwavering purpose.

Congratulations for choosing to unlock a better life. Only you can stop yourself. Go on, take action now and unleash your best self!

www.ingramcontent.com/pod-product-compliance
Lightning Source LLC
Chambersburg PA
CBHW070825260726
48660CB00005B/1989